Shifts

Shifts

THE JOURNAL
for Nurses by Nurses

Kay Kennedy ✿ Lucy Leclerc ✿ Susan Campis

NEW YORK

LONDON • NASHVILLE • MELBOURNE • VANCOUVER

Shifts
A Journal for Nurses by Nurses

© 2022 Kay Kennedy Lucy Leclerc Susan Campis

Published in New York, New York, by Morgan James Publishing. Morgan James is a trademark of Morgan James, LLC. www.MorganJamesPublishing.com

Morgan James BOGO™

A **FREE** ebook edition is available for you or a friend with the purchase of this print book.

CLEARLY SIGN YOUR NAME ABOVE

Instructions to claim your free ebook edition:
1. Visit MorganJamesBOGO.com
2. Sign your name CLEARLY in the space above
3. Complete the form and submit a photo of this entire page
4. You or your friend can download the ebook to your preferred device

ISBN 978-1-63195-528-0 paperback
ISBN 978-1-63195-530-3 hardcover
Library of Congress Control Number:
2021910784

Cover Design by:
Rachel Lopez
www.r2cdesign.com

Morgan James is a proud partner of Habitat for Humanity Peninsula and Greater Williamsburg. Partners in building since 2006.

Get involved today! Visit
MorganJamesPublishing.com/giving-back

There's about to be a shift
in your life.

WELCOME TO SHIFTS

Reflective journaling is a process used to help provide clarity around our thoughts, behaviors, and feelings related to experiences, concerns, and issues that occur daily. It is seen as a powerful and effective tool for self-management and well-being. Reflective journaling challenges us to contemplate meaningful questions and to reply with honest answers. It is not an easy process, because we open ourselves to the consequences of our actions. However, we also become aware of our strengths, our dreams, and our passions, which often leads us to discover what brings us true joy.

The practice of reflective journaling can be improved when there is some sort of framework to guide the reflective thought process. What if there was a journaling framework for nurses designed to mirror how nurses think, communicate, and process information?

Shifts is a journal designed for nurses by nurses. As the title implies, the practice of reflective thinking and reflective journaling will often cause a *Shift* in the way we perceive experiences and events occurring in our lives. Through reflective practice, we are provided the opportunity to shift perspective, shift attitude, and shift behavior, which creates a positive shift in our personal growth.

This journal uses an SBAR format, a familiar and standardized communication tool used in healthcare, and steers you to reflect first on your own health and well-being. The journaling process asks you

1

to identify and commit to an intention. The intention is used to help manifest the personal and professional goals and vision you have for yourself. The intention can be general or specific, but it needs to be positive in tone and easily adjustable. Everyone is unique. While one person might incorporate an intention into their way of being within 2-3 weeks, others might take 2-3 months or even a year! That means your intention might change month to month or it might stay the same. The journaling process will challenge you to reflect on how your experiences influence your intention.

The SBAR format for reflective journaling begins with **SITUATION**. Reflect on an experience or event, big or small, positive or negative, that impacted your day. What happened? When did it happen? Where did it happen? Were other people involved? After describing the situation in as much detail as you feel necessary, move your thoughts to the next step, **BACKGROUND**. Here, you are encouraged to focus on pertinent information relating to how your sense of well-being influenced the situation. For example, as you focus on self-care, or the physical aspects of well-being, ask yourself questions such as: Am I eating foods that are healthy and clean? Am I drinking plenty of fluids to keep me hydrated? Am I getting enough quality sleep? Am I exercising my body? As you begin to reflect on your mental health, ask yourself these questions: Do I take time out of each day to pause, breathe, and be present in the moment? Am I finding the time to nurture my relationships with friends and family? Self-compassion is an important facet of reflective journaling, so think about the following questions: Am I experiencing negative self-talk during my day? Did I expect perfection from myself today? What am I doing to stay mentally healthy? Did I do something in the past 24 hours that brought me joy? Finally, how self-aware did you feel today? What stressed you out? What made you happy or angry? How did your emotions impact you? How did your emotions impact others? Self-care means many things to many people but in simple terms, it means you taking care of you. We all know that we respond to situations based on how we feel physically, mentally, emotionally, and spiritually. It's OK to acknowledge that we might, at times, fail at self-care. It happens to the best of us. Reflective journaling should provide you with the acumen to see where those gaps in your self-care practice may lie.

In **ASSESSMENT**, you are encouraged to use your thoughts and insights to analyze and evaluate your situation. Ask yourself questions such as: What is really going on? What am I learning about myself? How does what I'm learning about myself align with my intention? Answering these questions in an honest and authentic way encourages an openness and vulnerability within yourself. The **RECOMMENDATIONS** portion challenges you to reflect on areas identified as strengths, as well as opportunities for growth. Developing a plan of action to address identified opportunities becomes the foundation for growth and development. Ask yourself the following questions: What would I do differently if this situation were to ever happen again? Where did I shine?

Go forth, reflect, and make a positive shift. It starts with you!

Your life doesn't improve with good luck, it improves with good intentions.

THE POWER OF INTENTION

I intend to...
- Give myself grace.
- Be kind.
- Be generous.
- Be positive.
- Forgive others and myself.
- Love unconditionally.
- Make someone smile every day.
- Prioritize self-care.
- Channel delight into my day, every day.
- Show up for myself.
- Be my authentic self.
- Go with the flow.
- Discover who I am and what I enjoy.
- Explore something I've never seen or done before.
- Talk to myself as if talking to my best friend.
- Dance like no one's watching!
- Live unapologetically.
- Live wholeheartedly.
- Find beauty in every day.
- Be present in the moment.
- Be authentically present.
- Create and maintain boundaries.
- Do something every day that brings me joy.
- Create simplicity and peacefulness in my day, every day.
- Be accepting of my and others' imperfections.
- Hear the whole story instead of filling in the gaps (listen).
- Assume positive intent with others.
- Act with courage.
- Accept myself as enough.
- Be unafraid to try difficult things.
- Drink enough water.
- Look for the positive side in negative situations.
- Control what I can control.
- Face today's challenges with a calm mind and conviction.
- Awaken my creativity.
- Nourish my body with clean and healthy food.
- Develop the habit of exercise.
- Look for ways to fulfill my purpose.

FOR THE NEXT MONTH, MY INTENTION WILL BE TO...

BECAUSE...

Date:

Today, I recommit to **my intention**:

Situation:

Reflect on an experience or event, big or small, positive or negative, that impacted your day. What happened?

Background:

Pertinent information about how my sense of well-being influenced the situation:

Mind

Body

Spirit

Add some details.

Assessment:

What's really going on? What am I learning? How does this align with my intention?

Recommendations:

What would I do differently if this situation were to ever happen again? Where did I shine?

Today's action plan:

This is what I'm going to change (which could include my intention).

1.
2.

This is what I'm going to keep doing!

1.
2.

Nurse's Notes:

Date:

Today, I recommit to **my intention**:

Situation:

Reflect on an experience or event, big or small, positive or negative, that impacted your day. What happened?

Background:

Pertinent information about how my sense of well-being influenced the situation:

Mind

Body

Spirit

Add some details .

Assessment:
What's really going on? What am I learning? How does this align with my intention?

Recommendations:
What would I do differently if this situation were to ever happen again? Where did I shine?

Today's action plan:
This is what I'm going to change (which could include my intention).
1.
2.
This is what I'm going to keep doing!
1.
2.

Nurse's Notes:

Date:

Today, I recommit to **my intention**:

Situation:

Reflect on an experience or event, big or small, positive or negative, that impacted your day. What happened?

Background:

Pertinent information about how my sense of well-being influenced the situation:

Mind

Body

Spirit

Add some details.

Assessment:

What's really going on? What am I learning? How does this align with my intention?

Recommendations:

What would I do differently if this situation were to ever happen again? Where did I shine?

Today's action plan:

This is what I'm going to change (which could include my intention).

1.

2.

This is what I'm going to keep doing!

1.

2.

Nurse's Notes:

Date:

Today, I recommit to **my intention**:

Situation:

Reflect on an experience or event, big or small, positive or negative, that impacted your day. What happened?

Background:

Pertinent information about how my sense of well-being influenced the situation:

Mind

Body

Spirit

Add some details .

Assessment:
What's really going on? What am I learning? How does this align with my intention?

Recommendations:
What would I do differently if this situation were to ever happen again? Where did I shine?

Today's action plan:
This is what I'm going to change (which could include my intention).
1.
2.
This is what I'm going to keep doing!
1.
2.

Nurse's Notes:

Date:

Today, I recommit to **my intention**:

Situation:

Reflect on an experience or event, big or small, positive or negative, that impacted your day. What happened?

Background:

Pertinent information about how my sense of well-being influenced the situation:

Mind

Body

Spirit

Add some details.

Assessment:
What's really going on? What am I learning? How does this align with my intention?

Recommendations:
What would I do differently if this situation were to ever happen again? Where did I shine?

Today's action plan:
This is what I'm going to change (which could include my intention).
1.
2.
This is what I'm going to keep doing!
1.
2.

Nurse's Notes:

Date:

Today, I recommit to **my intention**:

Situation:

Reflect on an experience or event, big or small, positive or negative, that impacted your day. What happened?

Background:

Pertinent information about how my sense of well-being influenced the situation:

Mind

Body

Spirit

Add some details.

Assessment:

What's really going on? What am I learning? How does this align with my intention?

Recommendations:

What would I do differently if this situation were to ever happen again? Where did I shine?

Today's action plan:

This is what I'm going to change (which could include my intention).
1.
2.

This is what I'm going to keep doing!
1.
2.

Nurse's Notes:

Date:

Today, I recommit to **my intention**:

Situation:

Reflect on an experience or event, big or small, positive or negative, that impacted your day. What happened?

Background:

Pertinent information about how my sense of well-being influenced the situation:

Mind

Body

Spirit

Add some details .

Assessment:

What's really going on? What am I learning? How does this align with my intention?

Recommendations:

What would I do differently if this situation were to ever happen again? Where did I shine?

Today's action plan:

This is what I'm going to change (which could include my intention).

1.

2.

This is what I'm going to keep doing!

1.

2.

Nurse's Notes:

Date:

Today, I recommit to **my intention**:

Situation:

Reflect on an experience or event, big or small, positive or negative, that impacted your day. What happened?

Background:

Pertinent information about how my sense of well-being influenced the situation:

      Mind

      Body

      Spirit

Add some details .

Assessment:
What's really going on? What am I learning? How does this align with my intention?

Recommendations:
What would I do differently if this situation were to ever happen again? Where did I shine?

Today's action plan:
This is what I'm going to change (which could include my intention).
1.
2.
This is what I'm going to keep doing!
1.
2.

Nurse's Notes:

Date:

Today, I recommit to **my intention**:

Situation:

Reflect on an experience or event, big or small, positive or negative, that impacted your day. What happened?

Background:

Pertinent information about how my sense of well-being influenced the situation:

Mind

Body

Spirit

Add some details.

Assessment:

What's really going on? What am I learning? How does this align with my intention?

Recommendations:

What would I do differently if this situation were to ever happen again? Where did I shine?

Today's action plan:

This is what I'm going to change (which could include my intention).

1.
2.

This is what I'm going to keep doing!

1.
2.

Nurse's Notes:

Date:
Today, I recommit to **my intention**:

Situation:
Reflect on an experience or event, big or small, positive or negative, that impacted your day. What happened?

Background:
Pertinent information about how my sense of well-being influenced the situation:

Mind

Body

Spirit

Add some details.

Assessment:
What's really going on? What am I learning? How does this align with my intention?

.   .   .   .
.   .   .   .
.   .   .   .
.   .   .   .
.   .   .   .

Recommendations:
What would I do differently if this situation were to ever happen again? Where did I shine?

.   .   .   .
.   .   .   .
.   .   .   .

Today's action plan:
This is what I'm going to change (which could include my intention).
1.   .   .   .   .
2.   .   .   .   .
This is what I'm going to keep doing!
1.   .   .   .   .
2.   .   .   .   .

Nurse's Notes:

.   .   .   .
.   .   .   .
.   .   .   .
.   .   .   .
.   .   .   .
.   .   .   .
.   .   .   .
.   .   .   .

Date:

Today, I recommit to **my intention**:

Situation:

Reflect on an experience or event, big or small, positive or negative, that impacted your day. What happened?

Background:

Pertinent information about how my sense of well-being influenced the situation:

Mind

Body

Spirit

Add some details.

Assessment:
What's really going on? What am I learning? How does this align with my intention?

Recommendations:
What would I do differently if this situation were to ever happen again? Where did I shine?

Today's action plan:
This is what I'm going to change (which could include my intention).
1.
2.
This is what I'm going to keep doing!
1.
2.

Nurse's Notes:

Date:

Today, I recommit to **my intention**:

.   .   .   .

.   .   .   .

Situation:

Reflect on an experience or event, big or small, positive or negative, that impacted your day. What happened?

.   .   .   .

.   .   .   .

.   .   .   .

.   .   .   .

Background:

Pertinent information about how my sense of well-being influenced the situation:

Mind   .   .   .   .

.   .   .   .

.   .   .   .

.   .   .   .

Body   .   .   .   .

.   .   .   .

.   .   .   .

.   .   .   .

Spirit   .   .   .   .

.   .   .   .

.   .   .   .

Add some details .   .   .   .

.   .   .   .

.   .   .   .

.   .   .   .

.   .   .   .

Assessment:
What's really going on? What am I learning? How does this align with my intention?

Recommendations:
What would I do differently if this situation were to ever happen again? Where did I shine?

Today's action plan:
This is what I'm going to change (which could include my intention).
1.
2.
This is what I'm going to keep doing!
1.
2.

Nurse's Notes:

Date:

Today, I recommit to **my intention**:

Situation:

Reflect on an experience or event, big or small, positive or negative, that impacted your day. What happened?

Background:

Pertinent information about how my sense of well-being influenced the situation:

Mind

Body

Spirit

Add some details .

Assessment:

What's really going on? What am I learning? How does this align with my intention?

.   .   .   .
.   .   .   .
.   .   .   .
.   .   .   .
.   .   .   .

Recommendations:

What would I do differently if this situation were to ever happen again? Where did I shine?

.   .   .   .
.   .   .   .
.   .   .   .

Today's action plan:

This is what I'm going to change (which could include my intention).

1.   .   .   .   .
2.   .   .   .   .

This is what I'm going to keep doing!

1.   .   .   .   .
2.   .   .   .   .

Nurse's Notes:

.   .   .   .
.   .   .   .
.   .   .   .
.   .   .   .
.   .   .   .
.   .   .   .
.   .   .   .
.   .   .   .

Date:

Today, I recommit to **my intention**:

Situation:

Reflect on an experience or event, big or small, positive or negative, that impacted your day. What happened?

Background:

Pertinent information about how my sense of well-being influenced the situation:

Mind

Body

Spirit

Add some details.

Assessment:
What's really going on? What am I learning? How does this align with my intention?

Recommendations:
What would I do differently if this situation were to ever happen again? Where did I shine?

Today's action plan:
This is what I'm going to change (which could include my intention).
1.
2.
This is what I'm going to keep doing!
1.
2.

Nurse's Notes:

Date:

Today, I recommit to **my intention**:

Situation:

Reflect on an experience or event, big or small, positive or negative, that impacted your day. What happened?

Background:

Pertinent information about how my sense of well-being influenced the situation:

Mind

Body

Spirit

Add some details.

Assessment:

What's really going on? What am I learning? How does this align with my intention?

Recommendations:

What would I do differently if this situation were to ever happen again? Where did I shine?

Today's action plan:

This is what I'm going to change (which could include my intention).

1.
2.

This is what I'm going to keep doing!

1.
2.

Nurse's Notes:

Date:
Today, I recommit to **my intention**:

Situation:
Reflect on an experience or event, big or small, positive or negative, that impacted your day. What happened?

Background:
Pertinent information about how my sense of well-being influenced the situation:

Mind

Body

Spirit

Add some details.

Assessment:
What's really going on? What am I learning? How does this align with
my intention?

Recommendations:
What would I do differently if this situation were to ever happen
again? Where did I shine?

Today's action plan:
This is what I'm going to change (which could include my intention).
   1.
   2.
This is what I'm going to keep doing!
   1.
   2.

Nurse's Notes:

Date:

Today, I recommit to **my intention**:

Situation:

Reflect on an experience or event, big or small, positive or negative, that impacted your day. What happened?

Background:

Pertinent information about how my sense of well-being influenced the situation:

Mind

Body

Spirit

Add some details

Assessment:
What's really going on? What am I learning? How does this align with my intention?

Recommendations:
What would I do differently if this situation were to ever happen again? Where did I shine?

Today's action plan:
This is what I'm going to change (which could include my intention).

1.
2.

This is what I'm going to keep doing!

1.
2.

Nurse's Notes:

Date:

Today, I recommit to **my intention**:

Situation:

Reflect on an experience or event, big or small, positive or negative, that impacted your day. What happened?

Background:

Pertinent information about how my sense of well-being influenced the situation:

Mind

Body

Spirit

Add some details .

Assessment:

What's really going on? What am I learning? How does this align with my intention?

.   .   .   .

.   .   .   .

.   .   .   .

.   .   .   .

.   .   .   .

Recommendations:

What would I do differently if this situation were to ever happen again? Where did I shine?

.   .   .   .

.   .   .   .

.   .   .   .

Today's action plan:

This is what I'm going to change (which could include my intention).

1.   .   .   .   .

2.   .   .   .   .

This is what I'm going to keep doing!

1.   .   .   .   .

2.   .   .   .   .

Nurse's Notes:

.   .   .   .

.   .   .   .

.   .   .   .

.   .   .   .

.   .   .   .

.   .   .   .

.   .   .   .

.   .   .   .

Date:

Today, I recommit to **my intention**:

Situation:

Reflect on an experience or event, big or small, positive or negative, that impacted your day. What happened?

Background:

Pertinent information about how my sense of well-being influenced the situation:

Mind

Body

Spirit

Add some details

Assessment:
What's really going on? What am I learning? How does this align with my intention?

Recommendations:
What would I do differently if this situation were to ever happen again? Where did I shine?

Today's action plan:
This is what I'm going to change (which could include my intention).
1.
2.
This is what I'm going to keep doing!
1.
2.

Nurse's Notes:

Date:

Today, I recommit to **my intention**:

Situation:

Reflect on an experience or event, big or small, positive or negative, that impacted your day. What happened?

Background:

Pertinent information about how my sense of well-being influenced the situation:

Mind

Body

Spirit

Add some details.

Assessment:

What's really going on? What am I learning? How does this align with my intention?

Recommendations:

What would I do differently if this situation were to ever happen again? Where did I shine?

Today's action plan:

This is what I'm going to change (which could include my intention).

1.
2.

This is what I'm going to keep doing!

1.
2.

Nurse's Notes:

Small changes each
day result in big wins.

THE POWER OF INTENTION

I intend to...
- Give myself grace.
- Be kind.
- Be generous.
- Be positive.
- Forgive others and myself.
- Love unconditionally.
- Make someone smile every day.
- Prioritize self-care.
- Channel delight into my day, every day.
- Show up for myself.
- Be my authentic self.
- Go with the flow.
- Discover who I am and what I enjoy.
- Explore something I've never seen or done before.
- Talk to myself as if talking to my best friend.
- Dance like no one's watching!
- Live unapologetically.
- Live wholeheartedly.
- Find beauty in every day.
- Be present in the moment.
- Be authentically present.
- Create and maintain boundaries.
- Do something every day that brings me joy.
- Create simplicity and peacefulness in my day, every day.
- Be accepting of my and others' imperfections.
- Hear the whole story instead of filling in the gaps (listen).
- Assume positive intent with others.
- Act with courage.
- Accept myself as enough.
- Be unafraid to try difficult things.
- Drink enough water.
- Look for the positive side in negative situations.
- Control what I can control.
- Face today's challenges with a calm mind and conviction.
- Awaken my creativity.
- Nourish my body with clean and healthy food.
- Develop the habit of exercise.
- Look for ways to fulfill my purpose.

FOR THE NEXT MONTH, MY INTENTION WILL BE TO...

BECAUSE...

Date:

Today, I recommit to **my intention**:

Situation:

Reflect on an experience or event, big or small, positive or negative, that impacted your day. What happened?

Background:

Pertinent information about how my sense of well-being influenced the situation:

Mind

Body

Spirit

Add some details.

Assessment:
What's really going on? What am I learning? How does this align with my intention?

Recommendations:
What would I do differently if this situation were to ever happen again? Where did I shine?

Today's action plan:
This is what I'm going to change (which could include my intention).

1.
2.

This is what I'm going to keep doing!

1.
2.

Nurse's Notes:

Date:

Today, I recommit to **my intention**:

Situation:

Reflect on an experience or event, big or small, positive or negative, that impacted your day. What happened?

Background:

Pertinent information about how my sense of well-being influenced the situation:

Mind

Body

Spirit

Add some details

Assessment:
What's really going on? What am I learning? How does this align with my intention?

Recommendations:
What would I do differently if this situation were to ever happen again? Where did I shine?

Today's action plan:
This is what I'm going to change (which could include my intention).
1.
2.
This is what I'm going to keep doing!
1.
2.

Nurse's Notes:

Date:

Today, I recommit to **my intention**:

Situation:

Reflect on an experience or event, big or small, positive or negative, that impacted your day. What happened?

Background:

Pertinent information about how my sense of well-being influenced the situation:

Mind

Body

Spirit

Add some details .

Assessment:

What's really going on? What am I learning? How does this align with my intention?

Recommendations:

What would I do differently if this situation were to ever happen again? Where did I shine?

Today's action plan:

This is what I'm going to change (which could include my intention).

1.

2.

This is what I'm going to keep doing!

1.

2.

Nurse's Notes:

Date:

Today, I recommit to **my intention**:

Situation:

Reflect on an experience or event, big or small, positive or negative, that impacted your day. What happened?

Background:

Pertinent information about how my sense of well-being influenced the situation:

Mind

Body

Spirit

Add some details.

Assessment:

What's really going on? What am I learning? How does this align with my intention?

.   .   .   .

.   .   .   .

.   .   .   .

.   .   .   .

.   .   .   .

Recommendations:

What would I do differently if this situation were to ever happen again? Where did I shine?

.   .   .   .

.   .   .   .

.   .   .   .

Today's action plan:

This is what I'm going to change (which could include my intention).

1.   .   .   .   .

2.   .   .   .   .

This is what I'm going to keep doing!

1.   .   .   .   .

2.   .   .   .   .

Nurse's Notes:

.   .   .   .

.   .   .   .

.   .   .   .

.   .   .   .

.   .   .   .

.   .   .   .

.   .   .   .

.   .   .   .

Date:

Today, I recommit to **my intention**:

Situation:

Reflect on an experience or event, big or small, positive or negative, that impacted your day. What happened?

Background:

Pertinent information about how my sense of well-being influenced the situation:

Mind

Body

Spirit

Add some details.

Assessment:
What's really going on? What am I learning? How does this align with my intention?

Recommendations:
What would I do differently if this situation were to ever happen again? Where did I shine?

Today's action plan:
This is what I'm going to change (which could include my intention).
1.
2.
This is what I'm going to keep doing!
1.
2.

Nurse's Notes:

Date:
Today, I recommit to **my intention**:

Situation:
Reflect on an experience or event, big or small, positive or negative, that impacted your day. What happened?

Background:
Pertinent information about how my sense of well-being influenced the situation:

Mind

Body

Spirit

Add some details

Assessment:
What's really going on? What am I learning? How does this align with my intention?

Recommendations:
What would I do differently if this situation were to ever happen again? Where did I shine?

Today's action plan:
This is what I'm going to change (which could include my intention).

1.
2.

This is what I'm going to keep doing!

1.
2.

Nurse's Notes:

Date:

Today, I recommit to **my intention**:

Situation:

Reflect on an experience or event, big or small, positive or negative, that impacted your day. What happened?

Background:

Pertinent information about how my sense of well-being influenced the situation:

Mind

Body

Spirit

Add some details .

Assessment:

What's really going on? What am I learning? How does this align with my intention?

Recommendations:

What would I do differently if this situation were to ever happen again? Where did I shine?

Today's action plan:

This is what I'm going to change (which could include my intention).

1.
2.

This is what I'm going to keep doing!

1.
2.

Nurse's Notes:

Date:

Today, I recommit to **my intention**:

.   .   .   .

.   .   .   .

Situation:

Reflect on an experience or event, big or small, positive or negative, that impacted your day. What happened?

.   .   .   .

.   .   .   .

.   .   .   .

.   .   .   .

Background:

Pertinent information about how my sense of well-being influenced the situation:

Mind   .   .   .   .

.   .   .   .

.   .   .   .

.   .   .   .

Body   .   .   .   .

.   .   .   .

.   .   .   .

.   .   .   .

Spirit   .   .   .   .

.   .   .   .

.   .   .   .

.   .   .   .

Add some details .   .   .   .

.   .   .   .

.   .   .   .

.   .   .   .

.   .   .   .

Assessment:
What's really going on? What am I learning? How does this align with my intention?

Recommendations:
What would I do differently if this situation were to ever happen again? Where did I shine?

Today's action plan:
This is what I'm going to change (which could include my intention).
    1.
    2.
This is what I'm going to keep doing!
    1.
    2.

Nurse's Notes:

Date:

Today, I recommit to **my intention**:

Situation:

Reflect on an experience or event, big or small, positive or negative, that impacted your day. What happened?

Background:

Pertinent information about how my sense of well-being influenced the situation:

Mind

Body

Spirit

Add some details .

Assessment:
What's really going on? What am I learning? How does this align with my intention?

Recommendations:
What would I do differently if this situation were to ever happen again? Where did I shine?

Today's action plan:
This is what I'm going to change (which could include my intention).

   1.

   2.

This is what I'm going to keep doing!

   1.

   2.

Nurse's Notes:

Date:

Today, I recommit to **my intention**:

Situation:

Reflect on an experience or event, big or small, positive or negative, that impacted your day. What happened?

Background:

Pertinent information about how my sense of well-being influenced the situation:

Mind

Body

Spirit

Add some details .

Assessment:

What's really going on? What am I learning? How does this align with my intention?

.   .   .   .

.   .   .   .

.   .   .   .

.   .   .   .

.   .   .   .

Recommendations:

What would I do differently if this situation were to ever happen again? Where did I shine?

.   .   .   .

.   .   .   .

.   .   .   .

Today's action plan:

This is what I'm going to change (which could include my intention).

1.   .   .   .   .

2.   .   .   .   .

This is what I'm going to keep doing!

1.   .   .   .   .

2.   .   .   .   .

Nurse's Notes:

.   .   .   .

.   .   .   .

.   .   .   .

.   .   .   .

.   .   .   .

.   .   .   .

.   .   .   .

.   .   .   .

Date:

Today, I recommit to **my intention**:

Situation:

Reflect on an experience or event, big or small, positive or negative, that impacted your day. What happened?

Background:

Pertinent information about how my sense of well-being influenced the situation:

Mind

Body

Spirit

Add some details .

Assessment:
What's really going on? What am I learning? How does this align with my intention?

Recommendations:
What would I do differently if this situation were to ever happen again? Where did I shine?

Today's action plan:
This is what I'm going to change (which could include my intention).
1.
2.
This is what I'm going to keep doing!
1.
2.

Nurse's Notes:

Date:

Today, I recommit to **my intention**:

Situation:

Reflect on an experience or event, big or small, positive or negative, that impacted your day. What happened?

Background:

Pertinent information about how my sense of well-being influenced the situation:

Mind

Body

Spirit

Add some details.

Assessment:
What's really going on? What am I learning? How does this align with my intention?

Recommendations:
What would I do differently if this situation were to ever happen again? Where did I shine?

Today's action plan:
This is what I'm going to change (which could include my intention).
1.
2.
This is what I'm going to keep doing!
1.
2.

Nurse's Notes:

Date:

Today, I recommit to **my intention**:

. . . .
. . . .

Situation:

Reflect on an experience or event, big or small, positive or negative, that impacted your day. What happened?

. . . .
. . . .
. . . .
. . . .

Background:

Pertinent information about how my sense of well-being influenced the situation:

Mind . . . .
. . . .
. . . .
. . . .
Body . . . .
. . . .
. . . .
. . . .
Spirit . . . .
. . . .
. . . .
Add some details . . . .
. . . .
. . . .
. . . .
. . . .

Assessment:
What's really going on? What am I learning? How does this align with my intention?

Recommendations:
What would I do differently if this situation were to ever happen again? Where did I shine?

Today's action plan:
This is what I'm going to change (which could include my intention).
    1.
    2.
This is what I'm going to keep doing!
    1.
    2.

Nurse's Notes:

Date:

Today, I recommit to **my intention**:

. . . .
. . . .

Situation:

Reflect on an experience or event, big or small, positive or negative, that impacted your day. What happened?

. . . .
. . . .
. . . .
. . . .

Background:

Pertinent information about how my sense of well-being influenced the situation:

Mind . . . .
. . . .
. . . .
. . . .

Body . . . .
. . . .
. . . .
. . . .

Spirit . . . .
. . . .
. . . .

Add some details . . . .
. . . .
. . . .
. . . .

Assessment:
What's really going on? What am I learning? How does this align with my intention?

Recommendations:
What would I do differently if this situation were to ever happen again? Where did I shine?

Today's action plan:
This is what I'm going to change (which could include my intention).

1.
2.

This is what I'm going to keep doing!

1.
2.

Nurse's Notes:

Date:

Today, I recommit to **my intention**:

Situation:

Reflect on an experience or event, big or small, positive or negative, that impacted your day. What happened?

Background:

Pertinent information about how my sense of well-being influenced the situation:

Mind

Body

Spirit

Add some details.

Assessment:
What's really going on? What am I learning? How does this align with my intention?

Recommendations:
What would I do differently if this situation were to ever happen again? Where did I shine?

Today's action plan:
This is what I'm going to change (which could include my intention).

1.
2.

This is what I'm going to keep doing!

1.
2.

Nurse's Notes:

Date:

Today, I recommit to **my intention**:

.   .   .   .

.   .   .   .

Situation:

Reflect on an experience or event, big or small, positive or negative, that impacted your day. What happened?

.   .   .   .

.   .   .   .

.   .   .   .

.   .   .   .

Background:

Pertinent information about how my sense of well-being influenced the situation:

Mind   .   .   .   .

.   .   .   .

.   .   .   .

.   .   .   .

Body   .   .   .   .

.   .   .   .

.   .   .   .

.   .   .   .

Spirit   .   .   .   .

.   .   .   .

.   .   .   .

Add some details .   .   .   .

.   .   .   .

.   .   .   .

.   .   .   .

.   .   .   .

Assessment:
What's really going on? What am I learning? How does this align with my intention?

Recommendations:
What would I do differently if this situation were to ever happen again? Where did I shine?

Today's action plan:
This is what I'm going to change (which could include my intention).
1.
2.
This is what I'm going to keep doing!
1.
2.

Nurse's Notes:

Date:

Today, I recommit to **my intention**:

Situation:

Reflect on an experience or event, big or small, positive or negative, that impacted your day. What happened?

Background:

Pertinent information about how my sense of well-being influenced the situation:

Mind

Body

Spirit

Add some details .

Assessment:
What's really going on? What am I learning? How does this align with my intention?

Recommendations:
What would I do differently if this situation were to ever happen again? Where did I shine?

Today's action plan:
This is what I'm going to change (which could include my intention).
1.
2.
This is what I'm going to keep doing!
1.
2.

Nurse's Notes:

Date:

Today, I recommit to **my intention**:

Situation:

Reflect on an experience or event, big or small, positive or negative, that impacted your day. What happened?

Background:

Pertinent information about how my sense of well-being influenced the situation:

Mind

Body

Spirit

Add some details

Assessment:

What's really going on? What am I learning? How does this align with my intention?

. . . .

. . . .

. . . .

. . . .

. . . .

Recommendations:

What would I do differently if this situation were to ever happen again? Where did I shine?

. . . .

. . . .

. . . .

Today's action plan:

This is what I'm going to change (which could include my intention).

1. . . . .
2. . . . .

This is what I'm going to keep doing!

1. . . . .
2. . . . .

Nurse's Notes:

. . . .

. . . .

. . . .

. . . .

. . . .

. . . .

. . . .

. . . .

Date:

Today, I recommit to **my intention**:

Situation:

Reflect on an experience or event, big or small, positive or negative, that impacted your day. What happened?

Background:

Pertinent information about how my sense of well-being influenced the situation:

Mind

Body

Spirit

Add some details .

Assessment:

What's really going on? What am I learning? How does this align with my intention?

Recommendations:

What would I do differently if this situation were to ever happen again? Where did I shine?

Today's action plan:

This is what I'm going to change (which could include my intention).

1.

2.

This is what I'm going to keep doing!

1.

2.

Nurse's Notes:

Date:

Today, I recommit to **my intention**:

Situation:

Reflect on an experience or event, big or small, positive or negative, that impacted your day. What happened?

Background:

Pertinent information about how my sense of well-being influenced the situation:

Mind

Body

Spirit

Add some details .

Assessment:
What's really going on? What am I learning? How does this align with my intention?

Recommendations:
What would I do differently if this situation were to ever happen again? Where did I shine?

Today's action plan:
This is what I'm going to change (which could include my intention).

1.
2.

This is what I'm going to keep doing!

1.
2.

Nurse's Notes:

How silent the woods
would be if only the
best birds sang.

THE POWER OF INTENTION

I intend to...
- Give myself grace.
- Be kind.
- Be generous.
- Be positive.
- Forgive others and myself.
- Love unconditionally.
- Make someone smile every day.
- Prioritize self-care.
- Channel delight into my day, every day.
- Show up for myself.
- Be my authentic self.
- Go with the flow.
- Discover who I am and what I enjoy.
- Explore something I've never seen or done before.
- Talk to myself as if talking to my best friend.
- Dance like no one's watching!
- Live unapologetically.
- Live wholeheartedly.
- Find beauty in every day.
- Be present in the moment.
- Be authentically present.
- Create and maintain boundaries.
- Do something every day that brings me joy.
- Create simplicity and peacefulness in my day, every day.
- Be accepting of my and others' imperfections.
- Hear the whole story instead of filling in the gaps (listen).
- Assume positive intent with others.
- Act with courage.
- Accept myself as enough.
- Be unafraid to try difficult things.
- Drink enough water.
- Look for the positive side in negative situations.
- Control what I can control.
- Face today's challenges with a calm mind and conviction.
- Awaken my creativity.
- Nourish my body with clean and healthy food.
- Develop the habit of exercise.
- Look for ways to fulfill my purpose.

FOR THE NEXT MONTH, MY INTENTION WILL BE TO...

BECAUSE...

Date:

Today, I recommit to **my intention**:

Situation:

Reflect on an experience or event, big or small, positive or negative, that impacted your day. What happened?

Background:

Pertinent information about how my sense of well-being influenced the situation:

Mind

Body

Spirit

Add some details.

Assessment:
What's really going on? What am I learning? How does this align with my intention?

Recommendations:
What would I do differently if this situation were to ever happen again? Where did I shine?

Today's action plan:
This is what I'm going to change (which could include my intention).
1.
2.
This is what I'm going to keep doing!
1.
2.

Nurse's Notes:

Date:

Today, I recommit to **my intention**:

Situation:

Reflect on an experience or event, big or small, positive or negative, that impacted your day. What happened?

Background:

Pertinent information about how my sense of well-being influenced the situation:

Mind

Body

Spirit

Add some details

Assessment:
What's really going on? What am I learning? How does this align with my intention?

Recommendations:
What would I do differently if this situation were to ever happen again? Where did I shine?

Today's action plan:
This is what I'm going to change (which could include my intention).

1.
2.

This is what I'm going to keep doing!

1.
2.

Nurse's Notes:

Date:

Today, I recommit to **my intention**:

Situation:

Reflect on an experience or event, big or small, positive or negative, that impacted your day. What happened?

Background:

Pertinent information about how my sense of well-being influenced the situation:

Mind

Body

Spirit

Add some details

Assessment:
What's really going on? What am I learning? How does this align with my intention?

Recommendations:
What would I do differently if this situation were to ever happen again? Where did I shine?

Today's action plan:
This is what I'm going to change (which could include my intention).
1.
2.
This is what I'm going to keep doing!
1.
2.

Nurse's Notes:

Date:

Today, I recommit to **my intention**:

Situation:

Reflect on an experience or event, big or small, positive or negative, that impacted your day. What happened?

Background:

Pertinent information about how my sense of well-being influenced the situation:

Mind

Body

Spirit

Add some details .

Assessment:
What's really going on? What am I learning? How does this align with my intention?

Recommendations:
What would I do differently if this situation were to ever happen again? Where did I shine?

Today's action plan:
This is what I'm going to change (which could include my intention).
   1.
   2.
This is what I'm going to keep doing!
   1.
   2.

Nurse's Notes:

Date:

Today, I recommit to **my intention**:

Situation:

Reflect on an experience or event, big or small, positive or negative, that impacted your day. What happened?

Background:

Pertinent information about how my sense of well-being influenced the situation:

Mind

Body

Spirit

Add some details .

Assessment:
What's really going on? What am I learning? How does this align with my intention?

Recommendations:
What would I do differently if this situation were to ever happen again? Where did I shine?

Today's action plan:
This is what I'm going to change (which could include my intention).

1.
2.

This is what I'm going to keep doing!

1.
2.

Nurse's Notes:

Date:

Today, I recommit to **my intention**:

Situation:

Reflect on an experience or event, big or small, positive or negative, that impacted your day. What happened?

Background:

Pertinent information about how my sense of well-being influenced the situation:

Mind

Body

Spirit

Add some details .

Assessment:

What's really going on? What am I learning? How does this align with my intention?

Recommendations:

What would I do differently if this situation were to ever happen again? Where did I shine?

Today's action plan:

This is what I'm going to change (which could include my intention).

1.

2.

This is what I'm going to keep doing!

1.

2.

Nurse's Notes:

Date:

Today, I recommit to **my intention**:

Situation:

Reflect on an experience or event, big or small, positive or negative, that impacted your day. What happened?

Background:

Pertinent information about how my sense of well-being influenced the situation:

Mind

Body

Spirit

Add some details .

Assessment:
What's really going on? What am I learning? How does this align with my intention?

Recommendations:
What would I do differently if this situation were to ever happen again? Where did I shine?

Today's action plan:
This is what I'm going to change (which could include my intention).
1.
2.
This is what I'm going to keep doing!
1.
2.

Nurse's Notes:

Date:

Today, I recommit to **my intention**:

Situation:

Reflect on an experience or event, big or small, positive or negative, that impacted your day. What happened?

Background:

Pertinent information about how my sense of well-being influenced the situation:

Mind

Body

Spirit

Add some details .

Assessment:
What's really going on? What am I learning? How does this align with my intention?

Recommendations:
What would I do differently if this situation were to ever happen again? Where did I shine?

Today's action plan:
This is what I'm going to change (which could include my intention).
1.
2.
This is what I'm going to keep doing!
1.
2.

Nurse's Notes:

Date:

Today, I recommit to **my intention**:

Situation:

Reflect on an experience or event, big or small, positive or negative, that impacted your day. What happened?

Background:

Pertinent information about how my sense of well-being influenced the situation:

Mind

Body

Spirit

Add some details .

Assessment:
What's really going on? What am I learning? How does this align with
my intention?

Recommendations:
What would I do differently if this situation were to ever happen
again? Where did I shine?

Today's action plan:
This is what I'm going to change (which could include my intention).
1.
2.
This is what I'm going to keep doing!
1.
2.

Nurse's Notes:

Date:

Today, I recommit to **my intention**:

Situation:

Reflect on an experience or event, big or small, positive or negative, that impacted your day. What happened?

Background:

Pertinent information about how my sense of well-being influenced the situation:

Mind

Body

Spirit

Add some details

Assessment:
What's really going on? What am I learning? How does this align with my intention?

.   .   .   .

.   .   .   .

.   .   .   .

.   .   .   .

.   .   .   .

Recommendations:
What would I do differently if this situation were to ever happen again? Where did I shine?

.   .   .   .

.   .   .   .

.   .   .   .

Today's action plan:
This is what I'm going to change (which could include my intention).

1.   .   .   .   .

2.   .   .   .   .

This is what I'm going to keep doing!

1.   .   .   .   .

2.   .   .   .   .

Nurse's Notes:

.   .   .   .

.   .   .   .

.   .   .   .

.   .   .   .

.   .   .   .

.   .   .   .

.   .   .   .

.   .   .   .

Date:

Today, I recommit to **my intention**:

Situation:

Reflect on an experience or event, big or small, positive or negative, that impacted your day. What happened?

Background:

Pertinent information about how my sense of well-being influenced the situation:

Mind

Body

Spirit

Add some details.

Assessment:
What's really going on? What am I learning? How does this align with my intention?

Recommendations:
What would I do differently if this situation were to ever happen again? Where did I shine?

Today's action plan:
This is what I'm going to change (which could include my intention).
1.
2.
This is what I'm going to keep doing!
1.
2.

Nurse's Notes:

Date:

Today, I recommit to **my intention**:

Situation:

Reflect on an experience or event, big or small, positive or negative, that impacted your day. What happened?

Background:

Pertinent information about how my sense of well-being influenced the situation:

Mind

Body

Spirit

Add some details .

Assessment:
What's really going on? What am I learning? How does this align with my intention?

Recommendations:
What would I do differently if this situation were to ever happen again? Where did I shine?

Today's action plan:
This is what I'm going to change (which could include my intention).
1.
2.
This is what I'm going to keep doing!
1.
2.

Nurse's Notes:

Date:

Today, I recommit to **my intention**:

Situation:

Reflect on an experience or event, big or small, positive or negative, that impacted your day. What happened?

Background:

Pertinent information about how my sense of well-being influenced the situation:

Mind

Body

Spirit

Add some details.

Assessment:
What's really going on? What am I learning? How does this align with my intention?

Recommendations:
What would I do differently if this situation were to ever happen again? Where did I shine?

Today's action plan:
This is what I'm going to change (which could include my intention).
1.
2.
This is what I'm going to keep doing!
1.
2.

Nurse's Notes:

Date:

Today, I recommit to **my intention**:

Situation:

Reflect on an experience or event, big or small, positive or negative, that impacted your day. What happened?

Background:

Pertinent information about how my sense of well-being influenced the situation:

Mind

Body

Spirit

Add some details.

Assessment:
What's really going on? What am I learning? How does this align with my intention?

Recommendations:
What would I do differently if this situation were to ever happen again? Where did I shine?

Today's action plan:
This is what I'm going to change (which could include my intention).
1.
2.
This is what I'm going to keep doing!
1.
2.

Nurse's Notes:

Date:

Today, I recommit to **my intention**:

Situation:

Reflect on an experience or event, big or small, positive or negative, that impacted your day. What happened?

Background:

Pertinent information about how my sense of well-being influenced the situation:

Mind

Body

Spirit

Add some details.

Assessment:
What's really going on? What am I learning? How does this align with my intention?

Recommendations:
What would I do differently if this situation were to ever happen again? Where did I shine?

Today's action plan:
This is what I'm going to change (which could include my intention).

1.

2.

This is what I'm going to keep doing!

1.

2.

Nurse's Notes:

Date:

Today, I recommit to **my intention**:

Situation:

Reflect on an experience or event, big or small, positive or negative, that impacted your day. What happened?

Background:

Pertinent information about how my sense of well-being influenced the situation:

Mind

Body

Spirit

Add some details .

Assessment:
What's really going on? What am I learning? How does this align with my intention?

Recommendations:
What would I do differently if this situation were to ever happen again? Where did I shine?

Today's action plan:
This is what I'm going to change (which could include my intention).
1.
2.
This is what I'm going to keep doing!
1.
2.

Nurse's Notes:

Date:

Today, I recommit to **my intention**:

Situation:

Reflect on an experience or event, big or small, positive or negative, that impacted your day. What happened?

Background:

Pertinent information about how my sense of well-being influenced the situation:

Mind

Body

Spirit

Add some details.

Assessment:

What's really going on? What am I learning? How does this align with my intention?

. . . .

. . . .

. . . .

. . . .

. . . .

Recommendations:

What would I do differently if this situation were to ever happen again? Where did I shine?

. . . .

. . . .

. . . .

Today's action plan:

This is what I'm going to change (which could include my intention).

1. . . . .

2. . . . .

This is what I'm going to keep doing!

1. . . . .

2. . . . .

Nurse's Notes:

. . . .

. . . .

. . . .

. . . .

. . . .

. . . .

. . . .

. . . .

Date:

Today, I recommit to **my intention**:

Situation:

Reflect on an experience or event, big or small, positive or negative, that impacted your day. What happened?

Background:

Pertinent information about how my sense of well-being influenced the situation:

Mind

Body

Spirit

Add some details.

Assessment:
What's really going on? What am I learning? How does this align with my intention?

.   .   .   .

.   .   .   .

.   .   .   .

.   .   .   .

.   .   .   .

Recommendations:
What would I do differently if this situation were to ever happen again? Where did I shine?

.   .   .   .

.   .   .   .

.   .   .   .

Today's action plan:
This is what I'm going to change (which could include my intention).
1.   .   .   .   .
2.   .   .   .   .

This is what I'm going to keep doing!
1.   .   .   .   .
2.   .   .   .   .

Nurse's Notes:

.   .   .   .

.   .   .   .

.   .   .   .

.   .   .   .

.   .   .   .

.   .   .   .

.   .   .   .

.   .   .   .

Date:

Today, I recommit to **my intention**:

Situation:

Reflect on an experience or event, big or small, positive or negative, that impacted your day. What happened?

Background:

Pertinent information about how my sense of well-being influenced the situation:

Mind

Body

Spirit

Add some details .

Assessment:

What's really going on? What am I learning? How does this align with my intention?

Recommendations:

What would I do differently if this situation were to ever happen again? Where did I shine?

Today's action plan:

This is what I'm going to change (which could include my intention).

1.
2.

This is what I'm going to keep doing!

1.
2.

Nurse's Notes:

Date:

Today, I recommit to **my intention**:

.   .   .   .

.   .   .   .

Situation:

Reflect on an experience or event, big or small, positive or negative, that impacted your day. What happened?

Background:

Pertinent information about how my sense of well-being influenced the situation:

Mind

Body

Spirit

Add some details.

Assessment:
What's really going on? What am I learning? How does this align with my intention?

Recommendations:
What would I do differently if this situation were to ever happen again? Where did I shine?

Today's action plan:
This is what I'm going to change (which could include my intention).

1.
2.

This is what I'm going to keep doing!

1.
2.

Nurse's Notes:

Inner peace begins
with self-awareness.

Nurses are in the unique position of caring for people during their most vulnerable time, making nursing a challenging, demanding, and emotion-filled profession. Many nurses place "care of self" at the bottom of a long list of "to dos."

Journaling can provide a safe space to decompress, reflect, and dream. It can be used as a tool to support the journey towards self-care, self-awareness, self-compassion, and mindfulness, providing greater insight into our thoughts and actions.

For more information, visit our website at www.uleadership.com.

It starts with you...

A free ebook edition is available with the purchase of this book.

To claim your free ebook edition:

Visit MorganJamesBOGO.com
Sign your name CLEARLY in the space
Complete the form and submit a photo of the entire copyright page
You or your friend can download the ebook to your preferred device

Morgan James
BOGO™

A **FREE** ebook edition is available for you or a friend with the purchase of this print book.

CLEARLY SIGN YOUR NAME ABOVE

Instructions to claim your free ebook edition:
1. Visit MorganJamesBOGO.com
2. Sign your name CLEARLY in the space above
3. Complete the form and submit a photo of this entire page
4. You or your friend can download the ebook to your preferred device

Print & Digital Together Forever.

Snap a photo

Free ebook

Read anywhere

www.ingramcontent.com/pod-product-compliance
Lightning Source LLC
Jackson TN
JSHW011927131224
75386JS00033B/1098